ENDLESS SCRIBBLES

MALAY PRAMANICK

INDIA • SINGAPORE • MALAYSIA

ISBN
Paperback 979-8-89744-655-1
Hardcase 979-8-89777-902-4

CONTENTS

B O O K   I I

ACKNOWLEDGEMENTS

1. I would like to express my unwavering gratitude to my parents for their support. They have been the pillars of my strength, providing me with the wisdom and values that have shaped me into the person I am today. It is because of them that I love reading so much.

2. I am indebted to the person who made me realize that, although life might throw some challenges, love is easy and effortless. She has helped me realize the value of moments and the gift of life once again. Her contributions to the anthology and my life are unparalleled.

3. I am appreciative of my friends, family, and supporters for believing in me and for their unshakable encouragement.

4. I am grateful to the people who have helped me see that it is not all bad and that there is still good left in the world.

5. Last but not least, I am thankful to my readers, critics, and publisher. I thank them for allowing my stories to become a part of their lives. Their insights and suggestions have helped me grow and improve as a writer.

BOOK I

For my love of poetry and songs

"And those who don't understand,
Get what they want to discover."

EBB

When a river flows at its brim
One can't ideate how it's deep,
When water begins to rescind
Only then gets to see the steep.

'Tis easy going when one's full,
Though fear might raise its head
Sailing into an unknown territory,
When the water does descend.

Then there's the dubiousness
If it's at the lowest for the time
Or if it's going to fall anymore
For tides do not wait for time.

The low tides are the real tests,
Struggles lie in flowing so low;
But seeing the river still flowing,
To the river, the sea does owe.

WAS I JEALOUS?

'Twas like any average morning,
Nothing was out of the blue;
I was cycling, going somewhere;
To where though, now no clue.

I do like to keep my eyes open,
As is needed to enjoy every ride;
I prefer taking the scenic routes,
As people, nature likes to hide.

I did come across a shabby man,
Might have been a homeless one;
He ate something out of a plastic,
After his carry bag was undone.

I cannot recollect him clearly
For I was fixated on his food,
I could not focus on my route,
The food did seem so good.

Happy was he, having his food;
Focused on food, didn't see me;
Would he have offered me some,
I ponder, had he then seen me?

Had he offered, to my gladness
I would have accepted the food;
What did in his food entice me?
Who's the culprit under the hood?

It might not have been enough
For two of us, or so it did seem;
I did not ask if he would share,
Was it my lack of self-esteem?

A FIRST DATE

Finally has she agreed for a date with me,

I'm gonna meet her for the very first time,

And when she sees, hope I don't look daffy,

How to hide this excitement and the chime?

What would she like? Maybe a movie date?

So romance in the movie blooms with ours;

Or should I ask to visit an amusement park?

Whatever be the matter, I'd get her flowers.

The excitement of anything for the first time,

Be it meeting her, hugging, or our first kiss,

Everything is hanging with a thin thread,

And with too much hope, things go abyss.

I hope she doesn't expect too much of me,

Even though it is a different kind of bliss,

Suppressing one's hopes in favor of reality;

In this elation, I hope things don't go amiss.

WHATEVER IT WAS

Whatever it was, I wanted to be about us;

There should be me moments and time,

But not indefinite, for frailty we exit stage,

You'd have got it, if our hearts did rhyme.

I did try my best, limited being a human,

How would my efforts lie, though I could?

Even some actions are liars, never was I,

Opened up for you to see, hoping you'd.

'Twas out of the blue, unintentional too,

What changed though, I was never a flirt.

I wish if you were rude, or did abuse me,

It was your inaction, which did really hurt.

It would have been a lot easier on me,

Even if it'd hurt, had you just hated me,

For hate proves one does thus matter,

That indifference is what I couldn't see.

I'd have stayed indefinitely beside you,

As I'd promised, if you were to keep me;

Actions speak volumes, it did not matter

If I were to stay, so why not just let it be?

BUSY

I know you are busy
Don't have any time
And have a lot to do,
Alas! I do miss you.

Tell me what I shall do
I wanna to talk to you;
Time has really flown
Since seed was sown.

Thanks to not meeting
My eyes cannot adore;
A ship sailed smoothly
On it I'm all but lonely.

I accept with difficulty
That you're this busy,
Todo list may be long
And excuses strong.

Is there no moment

Between a few tasks?

For I have work too,

But have time for you.

Things come and go

Even water at seas;

Never rescinds time,

Best it is, a gift prime.

JUST LIKE THAT

Hey, I'm going away, for I do annoy you,

And when you clearly had asked me to;

With this so-called love, what would I do,

If I cannot choose your wish over you?

Love happens, it happens just like that,

It is something, I have been unlucky at;

Acting as if it is not a big deal for me,

You will see, I will be gone just like that.

If you ever remember me, when I'm afar,

Please do remember what you had said,

It feels sad, though will be no complaint,

What are tears, nothing would be shed.

No more will I bother, already too much,

I will keep to myself, that I am good at,

Why'd I stay, I couldn't touch your heart,

Just for you, I will be gone, just like that.

COMPARISON

One of the easiest ways to hurt someone
Is to compare them with someone else;
Whatever be the intention, good or bad,
In one's memory, the comparison dwells.

No two persons are the same, nothing is,
Even an opportunity doesn't knock twice;
Every action has an associated reaction,
Similarly, a comparison also has a price.

Everything's different, even if very minute,
Between two, no matter what they claim,
Different people do learn in different ways,
Then how can the teaching be the same?

We can learn something from everyone,
Everyone's a genius, might be unaware,
Unexposed, of their areas of expertise,
It's to belittle them if one does compare.

A CHANCE

If you witness something unexpectedly
Give it a chance, it may be outstanding;
For even if it does seem vague at first,
It might turn out to be good, or be bad,
No matter what, it'd be an experience.

At times silence is the answer for one,
Neither it be any action nor any word,
No expression of the feelings would do.
Out of our comfort zone lies unknown,
Without any chance, may they be lost.

Don't be afraid to cry, give tears away,
It'll free your mind of sorrowful thoughts.
For things never end poetically, never;
They are made into songs as they end,
Some good ones were mere sad affairs.

Above everything, give love a chance,

To love, to be vulnerable, is indeed risky,

Feels like sailing into territory unknown,

Without any risk, is anything possible?

To love, one's to be lovable, to risk it all.

A BROKEN PROMISE

The worst thing about a broken promise,

A promise once made but been broken,

Is that it might make one feel so unworthy,

Unworthy of the thing they were promised.

At that moment, it's difficult not to feel bad,

One's situations do change, so do people,

Even what once meant, so do the values;

If not any, their mask might have dropped.

One's to understand, worth is inside them,

Why even look for any validation without?

I do agree that appreciations do feel good,

But if missing, the value remains the same.

It is not only about one it's been made to,

It also has something of the one making,

The values the person upholds or shows,

So just don't, even if it's easy to feel down.

BATTLES

Life is a play where battles abound,
Worst among them are the lost ones
Where wins the fear for losing them
Before one could pick up their guns.

The greatest ones have been unseen,
Many amongst aren't even spoken of,
May have failed in a test, lost money,
One might feel defeated in life or love.

Life is bigger than any incident, it is;
Life is a journey, and to love is to be;
The last one might have happened
To prepare for the future; we will see.

We do not know of all one's fighting,
Or about how many more lies ahead;
It doesn't take one much to be kind,
To a stranger fellow or to their stead.

LAUGHING

Some start with a smiley smile
While others burst loud and hard,
Everyone has got their own way,
'Tis the happiness that I regard.

Some do wear heart on sleeves,
I've seen people laugh very hard;
While others may not be so open,
Even laughing, they are on guard.

Laughter is but a good medicine,
Does some good to one's heart,
But when the going gets difficult
Keeping up a smile is an art.

Some do have to try a li'l harder,
I've also seen some laugh a lot;
Difficult are their unseen battles,
At the very verge, they're caught.

CHOICES

Depends on various things,

A relationship needs effort.

A feeling of belongingness,

Sharing a bond and a spark,

Harmony and understanding,

Do contribute on their part.

Effort needs to be there,

For there is no substitute.

A spark can start a journey,

And a bond can hold it far,

Doesn't that mean effort

Could be cut some slack.

People change, so do sparks.

Passive things can carry it,

Activeness is needed to go on.

The difference between these,

"We are so compatible," and

"I choose you," does say it all.

TAKEN FOR GRANTED

When one does get something,

Without even trying or asking,

'Tis easy for one to forget that

For the same, many are praying.

Acquired without or less effort,

Are the things we do value less;

One may have working hard,

With these things, did us bless.

If someone loves the ocean,

Does not mean should drown;

Criticism should be creative,

But easily one does put down.

With time we do tend to forget

The effort we had put and care,

To obtain things or be with one,

But without care, things do wear.

The living do get less flowers,

Way less than the ones dead;

Regret is greater than gratitude,

Why do we take one for granted?

A DATE TO REGRET

I have heard stories of various dates,
Perfect ones to horribly gone wrong;
Have heard some weird ones as well,
A terrible singer going to a sing along.

Some fun moments, to commitments,
Dates can offer a range of outcomes;
Nonetheless, they are an experience,
With experience, better one becomes.

Do not wait too long to ask them out,
Life takes sudden unexpected turns;
'Tis not always that we have the time
Think we have, late someone learns.

Worried of the cost of asking one out?
Gonna be a no, if you don't ask at all;
People regret dates they did not ask,
Above all, no regret is ever too small.

WORDS

There's something about words,
Something magical, enthralling,
Something that entices worlds,
But all we know, it's not the thing.

It's just not only prayers or chants,
I am talking about regular words;
Stitched into the fabric of music,
What's a song if not some words?

There are some abstract ones,
Which any of us can't even see,
Often carrying deep meanings,
From person to person, they vary.

Saying a thing calmly or loudly,
Does not make that real for more,
But it does put it out in the world,
And someday one might explore.

Coming from someone special,

Can mean a lot, just words a few,

Way more than the entire world,

Like the magic of one "I love you!"

PROBLEMS

Always there'll be barriers, even a few,
Some get bothered, seeing only a bit,
Some go ahead, walking the distance;
A life is to fight but only some go for it.

Big or small, there will be challenges,
There'll be twists, unexpected turns;
For life is to live and not to stagnate,
That's when the flowers turn to ferns.

To keep on, it's not that one can't rest,
Resting is okay, if one is determined;
Treading unknown paths ahead one,
Surprises and delight one might find.

Avoiding problems, one cannot grow,
In their absence, how can one strive?
They are a part of life, as all do know,
Facing and improving, we do truly live.

MATTERS

Does it? If you have held your ideals up,

How many stories you have played a role,

How much dedication you have shown,

If you've kept promises when they're gone,

if you cross someone's mind for any song,

Or some special place, of a particular town.

If are there walls, which one did not paint,

If one were to take a stand, but let it slide,

If one ceases to exist with their last breath;

Something to ponder, but do they matter?

All of us are self centered, aren't we really?

Not the center, it's the radius that matters.

THINGS I LOVE

One day, all of a while, I did find a note,

I had been listing down the things I love;

Have been through some difficult times,

Nonetheless, thank the heavens above.

I saw that it had some songs mentioned,

Most of which I still do hum, forgot a few,

Some for their meaning, some for music;

If I were to get it once again, none knew.

Friends, flowers, foods, animals, books,

Cartoons, places; it was a diverse one;

For people change and so do their likes,

It has to be updated but was never done.

It also had some moments mentioned,

Memories of smiling and offering help;

But it was far from being one complete,

Listing down, when did I forget myself?

IT'S IN THE PAST

One can't step into the same river twice;
With same offering, it's difficult to entice.
'Tis often said, a saint does have a past,
But then for others, why do we let it last?

I do not live in the past, that time is gone,
The person I used to be, is long bygone.
The dreams have changed deals for me,
As a wanderer does seek a home to be.

With lessons learnt, I have moved ahead,
Can't control or change it, even if I dread.
Good or bad, I had a past, for it I did pay;
It shaped me into the person I am today.

People change, for better or for worse,
Life continues while we look for a verse.
The past is gone, gone to be left as is it,
I am yet to understand, why judge by it?

TO LOVE

Exciting for it might sound, it's so easy,

Addicted to the idea of intoxicating love

Dangerous is any drunkenness; but,

When is it that we call it to be in love?

It is not just friendship, is love exactly?

There has to be love in a friendship,

Friendship in love, one's in the other;

Without either, people can easily trip.

May have something to do with beauty,

But it is never about looks or attraction;

Plentiful is literature of timeless loves,

Looks fade with time, so does passion.

To love is just to be, wish someone well,

To walk to the path, otherwise we won't;

Bestowing the power to destroy oneself,

To love one is to hope that they don't.

BOOK II

For someone special

"If not in this life, I will be yours in the kingdom come."

IS THIS WHAT LOVE FEELS LIKE?

After so rough a patch, how could one ease?
Just talking to her, did my nightmares cease!
The nights are still sleepless, it's not the same,
More than lost happiness, she helped reclaim.

Sometimes life can be better than a fairytale,
Though I am used to it, I don't want this to fail.
We didn't flirt, but for each other we did care;
I wish her well, but she's in my every prayer!

For the two of us, don't know what life'd unveil,
I just pray for the few days with her to prevail.
I was happy with her, I have never felt like that,
Even when beside each other, we had just sat.

What does she feel? She ever thinks of me?
I'd love to know if she was also happy by me.
Our connection was effortless, I'd felt so free,
Could share anything, from the sky to the sea.

That night with her, seemed bigger the moon.

I'd give anything to kiss her in the monsoon.

To have come across her, what good did I do?

She feels like the home I have never been to!

ON MY BENDED KNEE

I have always been a romantic,

But never have I feared so much,

To confess my feelings for you,

Even though I am sure as such.

I go to my bed, I just lay awake,

Feeling happy, with a wide smile,

As I only imagine being with you,

I've been in love with you awhile.

Thinking of you, I do fall asleep,

Even in sleep, I do dream of you;

We go on long drives, to places,

Even then, I fondly stare at you.

No matter however long we hug,

Lost in each other, we feel so free;

So many times, though in dreams,

I've proposed to you on one knee!

CONFESS?

Why has it become so difficult to imagine
To be with someone else, even to imagine,
When we have never even talked of love?
It's only you, being with you, I can think of.

If only I could get any hint from the above,
The perfect moment to confess my love,
I would definitely do, why would I stress?
Is it even love when I can't just confess?

Wish you all the happiness, wish you well,
Then what's stopping me, why can't I tell?
This is very unusual for someone like me,
Always heart is on my sleeve, one'd see.

Who is this new person, known to no one?
How did you even help a directionless one?
One can love, though not confess, it's true!
Look at me, I cannot say out loud but I do!

LABELLING IT

I am not used to this happiness
For I have never been so cared;
I'm used to be used and hatred,
'Tis too much for me, I'm scared.

People do ruin beautiful things,
Whatever this is, it is beautiful;
What kind of magic did you do
Entirety seems more beautiful.

Just let it be, whatever this is,
Labelling won't make it more;
You're someone for whom I'd
Fight with as well as fight for.

Calling won't change anything,
Just that I don't wanna jinx it;
I had been an unlucky fellow;
Till I met you, felt the opposite.

YOUR CRAZE

I smile like a crazy one
Whenever I think of you;
A few days of knowing
And I'm crazy about you.

Nothing fancy, nor forced,
Just felt so free with you;
I could share my sorrows,
'Twas that easy with you.

I think it wasn't only me,
Like me, free were you;
We could go on and on,
But someone'd call you.

Such short time together,
Still, I think only of you.
Nothing was amorous,
Yet I'm crazy about you.

Our hearts did connect,

I wanna hug, hold you.

You are my safe place,

In my mind, I run to you.

LOST IN MEMORIES

Moments make life worthwhile,
Memories are filled with them;
Though are not evenly spread,
Are more precious than any gem.

We hardly had met, so as to part,
Such a small window, just for us.
We had company, rarely alone,
And yet so freely, did we discuss.

I did not have any chance then
To drown myself in your eyes,
I did not have any intent though,
Each moment with you is a prize.

Didn't realise it sooner, I do now,
It was really calm, being with you.
Hoping we can meet again soon,
It seems as if I'm addicted to you.

THE MOON THAT NIGHT

I ate those fries though I was full,

For the fries were offered by you,

I'd have rejected, but I could not,

The next day I had to part with you.

After a while, we were left alone,

'Twas dark, if not for the moonlight;

As you showed the neighborhood

I just felt so blessed on that night.

The moon that night seemed bigger,

You agreed when I pointed that out;

Under the moon, we did connect,

And then someone called you out.

It wasn't a full moon, I didn't forget,

It was visible, yet you did mention;

Thought of parting brought me pain,

That part no one did ever mention.

GOODBYES

Goodbyes are no doubt difficult,
Especially from ones we adore;
Only a few days of connection,
But it made me thirsty for more.

Didn't wanna bade a goodbye,
I had a pile of excuses ready;
But time has a plan of its own,
And I had used some already.

When it was my time to leave,
To see me off, if she'd come,
I had hoped and I had prayed,
So happy was I, she did come.

I was so sad as well as happy,
I was getting to bade her bye;
'Tis too long till we meet again,
Eyes were teary, but I didn't cry.

Happy and the same time sad,

Among byes, hers was the last;

I have no idea if others noticed,

But had to struggle to drive past.

SO, I BLUSHED

Remember? As you were going to a store,

You did ask me if I would accompany you,

I said why not, I was anyways getting bored,

Though I like to drive, I was happy to let you.

After the work was done and we were free,

You asked me if I'd like to explore the city;

It wasn't a good idea with materials bought,

It was so foolish of me to reject it, I feel pity.

Enjoyed being a pillion rider, maybe my first,

We talked around, but did we have to rush?

Being back, you were asked who took whom,

I still don't know why, at that time, I did blush.

THE CONNECTION

An introvert I'm, for I rarely like to talk,
It's difficult to keep a discussion going;
Strangely, with you it wasn't the same,
Urge to talk to you was ever growing.

Joked around, had heartfelt laughter,
Could be just myself again around you;
From lighter moments to my sorrows,
I could share so much only with you.

We did not have much time together,
But it didn't take us long to get along;
Our connection was not a forced one,
It grew gradually and did grow strong.

Though I was too engrossed to realise,
Did you pick the vibe early, unlike me?
Might have realised our bond by now,
If so, none would feel as lucky as me.

HEAVEN'S GRACE

Meeting you was a blessing,
I feel heaven's been so kind;
Things were so easy with you,
For a friend in you did I find.

We did not talk or did converse,
'Twas our hearts, did we open;
I didn't think that was possible,
An introvert being outspoken.

A stranger was I, yet welcome,
In no time, we did get so close,
What's it if not heaven's grace?
'Tis you for me, my heart chose.

The way you laugh, your voice,
Like music still rings in my ears;
Those chances to look at you,
All gifts, even my parting tears.

ONLY FOR YOU

Of the path I've ploughed,
You have a fair idea now;
This path brought me here
To meet you, did it allow.

Though might seem crazy,
Again, with my open arms,
I'd tread through this path,
You do have such charms.

All those sleepless nights,
Heartbreaks, and the pain,
All paths lead me to you;
For you, I can bear again.

Beside you, I feel so calm,
Peacefully, I am at ease,
These outweigh the pain,
And my misery did freeze.

Were complete strangers,

Eye to eye, now we see;

I will face it all again, if it

Lets me get on one knee.

I'M SCARED

I'm known, rather very well known,

For a person who does ruin things;

For a fickle minded person am I,

One who does poetry and sings.

If I confess, I think you will accept,

That's not the thing I'm scared of,

For love lingers to be accepted;

With all my heart, it is you, I love.

I am scared, if you do accept me,

And of commitments I fall short,

Without realizing, if I do hurt you,

Or I fight you instead of support.

To err is human, and I am one,

One who loves you, with his all.

If we quarrel, please forgive me,

After all, in your arms I wanna fall.

DAYDREAMS

It's been ages since I last daydreamt,
I know, too much of anything is bad,
But they take me to you and help a lot;
Now that they have returned, I'm glad.

They do help one plan some moments,
When we can't choose who we fall for;
What's to stop me, I've already fallen,
Dreams make me yearn for you more.

This is a repeated one, we get close,
Tucking some hairs behind your ear,
I do gently kiss you on your forehead,
And hugging, I get lost in you my dear.

WALKING TOGETHER

We have spent some time together,
We've walked and we have stood,
Have we travelled, sharing a seat
And heartfelt laughter, all for good.

We've travelled, just the two of us,
Without you, anyway I was alone;
Been a trip of solitude to loneliness,
Not to the places that you've shown.

Been fond of those hands of yours,
I have seen various marks on them,
Shows the diligent person you are;
If only I could hold to caress them.

We have walked beside each other,
Our walks been interrupted as well;
Wanna walk with you, hand in hand,
Enough of distance, one could tell.

LIFE'S A JOURNEY

I am prepared to walk for miles,

For each and every step of yours;

If our hearts can meet, so can we;

Never will be distance a problem.

In the journey of life, we do tread,

Some paths are easy, some aren't;

To be happy is to try, to get going,

One may slow down, for some rest.

I have spent good days travelling,

Have been to places old and new;

Why can't I spend hours to travel,

Just to meet you, even for a few.

Secret to happy life is keeping up,

Change paths but never give up;

Why would I give up on my love?

Life's a journey, and so is to love.

A FEIGNING POET

'Tis never easy, such is the way of life,
To just survive and get things done;
Hope's the only thing keeping us alive,
When daily prayers go unanswered.

Days passed by, with no complaints,
Was not difficult to enjoy my solitude;
I'm someone who can go to cinemas,
To restaurants, on long drives alone.

Had never expected to come across
A person who'd blow me off ground;
Yet I came across you unexpectedly,
And taken by the sheer storm of love.

All know that a poet is difficult to trust,
To use their pen, a poet has to feign;
Confused would be all to know this,
In love, even poets can go insane…

IMPERFECTIONS

I like your imperfections, to see them,

Not to tease you, I am also the same;

I'd like to see if you get angry for that,

I love the real you, can't you feel that?

All your being, and not the idea of you,

Yes, including all the imperfections too.

I'm all yours, why would I ever judge?

Don't you understand a gentle nudge?

You being in the moment, sets me free,

Not worrying about the world, I do see.

I'd like to dance with you, it'd be ours,

I would like to go on and on, for hours.

I'd find pleasure in singing with you,

Especially when the lyrics forget you;

I like your imperfections, to see them,

Only to ensure that we are the same!

SO EXCITED

Closeness confuses like anything,

With pain, increases the longings;

Some distance does some good,

It helps one validate their feelings.

Next time I meet her, I'll be sure

Of my feelings and surely of me;

I'll work on hiding my excitement,

After so long, so close will we be.

What'll happen to my daydreams?

They are always about her only.

I might be able to discern those,

Maybe make 'em feel a li'l lonely.

With this excitement to meet her,

I hope I don't make a fool of me;

For so long, we have been so far;

After eons, it's my love I will see.

BIDDING BYES

Act of not closing the door as soon as someone leaves,
Waiting until one's been too far to hear the door close,
Or waiting to see if that person does turn around to look,
What's that if not affection all the consideration shows?

But when apart, we close the door as soon as possible,
The person leaving doesn't care enough to turn around,
Perhaps, some get so sure of it or do they get used to it,
To busyness or annoyance, affection does lose ground.

It's okay if we miss once or twice, as long as not regular,
Overwhelmed once in a while, but is our affection strong.
I do want to greet you at the door whenever it's possible,
One goodbye was so difficult, it's together we do belong.

EFFORTS

One has to work, sometimes hard,
If one wants to achieve something,
Or to show a person or to the world,
Fruits of that, happiness does bring.

Always actions do speak volumes,
More than words, they can speak;
That evening, also tired were you,
Yet you cooked, making me weak.

'Twas as if we cared more for other,
Don't even think to spare hours few;
Far from an idler, a workaholic am I,
Yet happy to miss a day just for you.

Regarding you, things are that easy,
How is that I don't even have to try?
Everything does seem so effortless,
So effortlessly do we see eye to eye.

CRAZY MORNINGS

I wanna wake up beside you, every day,
Look at you with your hair being a mess,
And adoring you in every possible way,
"I've been in love with you", I'd confess.

With your eyes barely open, but angry,
I'll irritate you and tease you playfully,
Our voice cracking, we being sleepy,
We would fight but then kiss gracefully.

The best way to start a day, is with you,
Everyday won't be same, but can start,
Excuses won't matter, nor will distance,
You have and will always own my heart.

RED ROSES

I would have to gift you flowers soon,
I'd offer you a wild one if not a rose;
I know the significance of a red one,
But the burden of that morning grows.

That morning, I trimmed two roses,
I didn't know what to do with them,
If anything like that happens again,
You will see, it won't be the same.

Got to spend so much time together,
Could've easily offered you one rose.
I don't regret, for I also did not know,
If so, I would have offered you those.

To get one, I might have to try hard,
For I do not know the place, I'm new;
And if I can't, believe it's in my heart,
What's a flower, my heart's with you.

A PILLION RIDER

I love scooters, and do love bikes,
I even go on long drives all alone.
To drive, I do not let anyone else,
The driver's seat was my throne.

Then on a decisive day, I did let,
Though you did offer me to drive;
Wearily I did decline, 'twas a bliss,
As your pillion rider, I felt so alive!

You recollected a funny incident,
And we did have a heartfelt laugh;
With that, my weariness was gone;
I fell in love, the way you did laugh.

After our work was accomplished,
Could have roamed, we had time,
Kept my distance for I didn't know;
I'll hug you from the back, next time.

A MYSTERY

You are the most beautiful mystery

I've come across, I wanna confess;

You are so gorgeous yet courteous,

Before I met you, I was living in vain.

Mine is a mind with a scientific blend,

I love puzzles and solving mysteries;

Yet this mystery, wanna call my own,

For only with you, I can truly do live.

There are things that can only be felt,

Things that cannot be understood,

Like the way we bonded, I'd relish it,

If I'm lucky enough to be beside you.

The one of life, will I drink to the lees,

The mystery of love, I do wanna live,

And your mystery, I'm already in love;

Coming across was the gift of my life.

YOU DID CATCH MY EYE

Tired was I, and I couldn't appreciate,
You are so beautiful and so gorgeous,
I couldn't stare though I was stunned,
But I melted seeing you so courteous.

'Twas quite clear, the evening we met,
Tired was I, you were not keeping well,
I had to travel, you had loads of work,
Wasn't for the looks but one could tell.

'Tis difficult to say if two'd get along;
Why the person for whom we'd met,
Intelligent though, I think I do know,
Tried to keep from me, you a secret.

I am a person for efforts, and for vibes,
Never for looks, but for you I did sigh;
It was not exactly a love at first sight,
But that evening you did catch my eye.

THE BEST KEPT SECRET

I didn't even know that you existed,
'Twas not very long before we met;
Could have missed but if intentional,
It was indeed a very well-kept secret.

Wanna thank with everything I have,
Thank the person for introducing us;
The secrecy might have added to it,
And so, the thrill was increased thus.

Then, I did not even know your name,
But you did know a little bit about me;
Careless, unaware of your existence,
Was awestruck the moment I did see.

You are so smart, you are so alluring,
Didn't know it'd get to this, as we met;
Few moments were enough to know,
You were indeed the best kept secret.

LIVE BY YOU

I can survive if deprived of you,

It's just that I want to live by you.

Every day, want you by my side,

'Tis you, in my heart does reside.

I have sighed while I was away;

Will make this choice every day,

The choice of being in your life;

I want you for the rest of my life.

I had heard, home isn't a place,

I got to feel that for your grace;

In you, found peace and a friend,

In your bliss, mine does depend.

I wanna walk by you, hold you,

You do understand, don't you?

I do vow to build a life with you,

Till death do us part, live by you.

TO GROW

In this ever-changing world,

Not changing is not an option;

Everything grows, everyone,

Not growing old isn't an option.

Growing up is but a choice,

So is to grow in love or to part;

Interesting is to notice people

So in love, some grow apart.

I do want for us to grow in love;

I wanna be, and grow, with you,

To enjoy my life with you, and

To grow old together with you,

When the dusts do settle,

I will still be fixated on you,

I'll be used to being with you;

I do wanna grow old with you.

DULL DAYS

Love can only be bestowed upon,
It can never be asked for or begged;
Though I have heard it several times,
Now I understand what they meant.

Fate has its own weird plans for us;
I wasn't looking for, yet I fell for you;
Whatever happens, just know that
My heart will always belong to you.

'Tis never about holding one's hands,
It's not about the shoulder to lean on,
But when the situations get difficult,
'Tis just being together and going on.

Love is not for so called special days,
Mundane days will be in the abound,
Dull days would try to weigh us down,
It'd be our tests to turn them around.

With you everything seems so easy,

Yet deep down I am a little scared;

Just trust me, through thick and thin,

To hold your hands, I am prepared.

ABOUT THE POET

Malay Pramanick lives in Kharagpur, a town in West Bengal, India, away from the hullabaloo and tussles of city life. He completed his graduation [B.Tech(H)] as well as his post-graduation [MS(R)] from the Department of Computer Science and Engineering, IIT Kharagpur. Born to Bengali parents, he is a data scientist with a passion for poetry. He believes that engineering is a noble pursuit but lives for art, romance, and love. He is dedicated to finding a verse to contribute to the ongoing powerful play of life. The verses might be his identity and could help others see the world through his eyes.